The Job

Eric T. Whitfield

BeachHouse Books

Chesterfield Missouri USA

BeachHouse
Books

www.beachhousebooks.com

Copyright

Graphics Credits:

The cover is a collaborative effort between Eric Whitfield and Dr. Bud Banis, based on an original photograph by Eric T. Whitfield.

Publication date October, 2001First Printing, october, 2001

ISBN 1-888725-68-0 BeachHouse Books Edition

ISBN 1-888725-69-9 MacroPrintBooks Edition

Library of Congress Cataloging-in-Publication Data

Whitfield, Eric T., 1972-

The job / Eric T. Whitfield.

p. cm.

ISBN 1-888725-68-0 (pbk : alk. paper) -- ISBN 1-888725-69-9 (pbk. : large print : alk. paper)

1. Grandfathers--Death--Fiction. I. Title.

PS3623.H585 J63 2001

813'.6--dc21   2001006236

BeachHouse Books

BeachHouse Books an Imprint of

Science & Humanities Press

PO Box 7151
Chesterfield, MO 63006-7151
(636) 394-4950

www.beachhousebooks.com

Dedication

For Grandpa and James—

wherever you may be.

Acknowledgements

I would like to extend a very special thank you to Cynthia V. for all your help, to PHS faculty Gary P., Mike C., & Nancy G. for your undying faith when I needed it most, to all my friends, to my family, without whom I cringe to think where I might be, and to my beautiful wife, Jaclyn, my friend, my love, my savior. I love you all.

A personal note from the Publisher:

When the student is ready, the teacher will appear.

I was particularly ready at the time Eric Whitfield shared this book—his first—with me.

My father-in-law had just died, and my wife, my daughters and I were in Wyoming for his funeral. Andy was a good friend. I'll always remember his gentle support throughout the years of joys and trauma we shared—but he had suffered. It was Andy's time to go—and Death came as a friend.

Harold Kushner's two books—*When Bad Things Happen to Good People*, and *How Good Do We Have to Be*—comforted me. Kushner observed that "Our memories give immortality to those we love."

Relationships don't die as our bodies do.

Eric Whitfield's *The Job* is an extraordinarily poignant vehicle for this message. As I read this short book, threads of imagery began to pull together in the middle and when I came to the end, the message hit home, as an emotional wave I should have seen building engulfed me.

There is a purpose and a time for everything.

If you have lost someone close to you, it is a time for you to read *The Job,* or perhaps it is a time to give this book to someone you love.

Robert J. Banis, PhD
St. Louis Missouri, July, 2001

The Job

Eric T. Whitfield

Grandpa's fingers drummed out a beat on the dashboard

as we drove down the road, undoubtedly to accompany the Big Band I was sure was happily playing in his head. Somehow, though silent to my ears, Grandpa's music always seemed tremendously audible to my soul. I could watch his leg bounce and hear the piano bang away, see his thumb strike the wheel in perfect time with the stand-up bass that now found a venue within my head as well. Grandpa would glance over at me knowingly, wink so quickly I would wonder if I saw it at all, and without a word, the two of us would roll down the road swinging to our own personal jazz concert. The silent music was so powerful, so emotional, it left a lump in my throat. The silence would not be broken until we came to a stop in the driveway of Grandma and Grandpa's house, concluding the concert. "Watch your noodle," he would say as I climbed out of the car.

Chapter I

Inside the house, Christmas was alive. The smells of Grandma's culinary artwork tickled my nostrils, teasing my appetite, and the air was filled with sounds of family. If I took the time to listen, to isolate each sound from the goulash of noise, perhaps I would hear young cousins laughing and fighting, and laughing again because they couldn't decide which was more fulfilling at the moment. Or I would hear my uncle telling a joke or maybe a story about his latest project in the garage and the laughter that always seemed to flow from his immediate vicinity. I would hear moms, spanning generations, scolding their children or babying them as seen fit by the eyes of the eternal mommy within each of them. And of course I would hear the sounds of subtle disagreements, never quite developing into arguments, between the grown-ups who tried desperately to hide their annoyance behind forced smiles, all while their toes curled inside their shoes. The sounds of family. Folks were split up into small clubs throughout the house. Grandma, apron-clad, stayed close to the kitchen. It always amazed me to see how many things she could do at once in the kitchen and still be a part of conversation and peace keeping. I will never know how Grandma functioned so efficiently while having to climb over people crowding her working area. The kitchen and the dining room were separated by a countertop cluttered with bar staples such as bourbon and vodka, whisky, vermouth, various mixers, and of course the signature bowl of nuts. This was a popular hangout with people, either standing in the kitchen or along the outskirts of the dining room, maintaining easy access to the Christmas cheer the bottles contained. The kids would usually, upon arrival, escape the grown-ups. They would head straight for the family room, the TV room as it was more commonly and perhaps more appropriately called. The TV room also played host to the Christmas tree. It was beautiful. Decorations of all colors hung from the branches, brilliant glass balls reflecting a slightly distorted version of the world in which I found myself--a world I secretly wondered about. Lights twinkled and beckoned and soon the cousins were on all fours, like dogs sniffing out new territory. Little eyes scanned the gifts that appeared to be strategically placed as if each package was a crucial piece to the holiday puzzle. Eventually, all the gifts were accounted for and each cousin knew who got the big one by the coffee table and who got the squishy soft package in the corner. This squishy soft package must be under all family Christmas trees, I am convinced of it. It is surely from a great-aunt who is never physically present but who leaves the telltale package with grandmas each year to be distributed. The cousins know exactly why this mystery aunt is never present, and if grown-ups thought back to the horribly ugly article of clothing that inevitably emerged from the squishy soft package found under their childhood Christmas trees, they would know exactly why as well.

Upon completion of the Christmas gift investigation and inventory, the cousins found their seats around the television and clicked it on. During this TV time, the cousins would get reacquainted with one another, overcoming any awkwardness that may have developed since the last gathering. Once this was accomplished, they would descend to the basement where the grown-ups had less immediate access. Here, age gaps melted away and labels held in the world outside of Grandma's disintegrated, rendering all equal. I do not confine the cousins to an age category because I believe that this ritual continues regardless of age--although as the cousins grow older, less time is devoted to basement roughhousing.

The men compete, though not admittedly, for the loudest laugh while gathered around the holiday cheer. The women lean over Grandma's nativity, a glorious display of rolling hills and quaint little villages surrounding the manger where the baby Jesus lays. They are always so impressed, even moved, by the tabletop time traveler. A string of small white lights snakes through Grandma's version of Bethlehem, past the shepherd in the field with his flock, past the baker who carefully removes his loaf from the stone hearth on a wooden paddle. Villagers and animals and, above all, the distinct sensation of Christmas. I watch as mommies and aunts point and smile and marvel at the display.

I observed each of these groups and could virtually predict behavior and dialogue, though I never felt to be a part of any of them. I wasn't interested in the sports and politics that peppered the exchange in the "manly-man club." Throughout the years, I felt too young, too old, or simply too different to be accepted as a part of the "kids' club." There were, of course, the women, but again, I just didn't fit comfortably. Excuse me, can somebody please point me toward the 'awkward, not sure how to be a part of the family and don't know what to talk about club'? Which corner are they meeting in?

Then I would see Grandpa. Grandpa used to sit just outside the Christmas playing field, proudly watching his family while he sipped his Manhattan. I would get a soda in a short plastic cup--not because I was thirsty but because of its therapeutic value, as it gave me something to do with my hands, something to look at--and I would go to sit beside Grandpa. It's odd, I know, that I would need such a security blanket while sitting with my own grandfather, but I seemed to always find myself in a state of discomfort at these family gatherings.

It wasn't only the family gatherings prompting my discomfort this year, however. Grandpa had recently been diagnosed with leukemia. I must admit, initially, the diagnosis didn't mean a great deal to me. After all, people are diagnosed with terrible illnesses everyday and in the end walk away as healthy as a horse. And besides, since the diagnosis, Grandpa seemed fine, further supporting my lack of concern.

I placed my cup on the table, grasped each pant leg with a thumb and forefinger just above the knee, gave a little tug, and settled into the chair by my grandfather.

"Hey," he greeted as I reached for my security blanket.

"Hey," I replied and looked up at my grandpa. As his lips met his glass, I looked at my grandfather as a living, breathing oxymoron. His face, swollen from steroids, reminded me of a blowfish, his pudgy, rounded cheeks hugging his mouth. Yet, his left wrist, the wrist upon which he wore his watch, had become so skinny with illness that the watch, now on its smallest band setting, had to be worn over the thick cotton/wool blended cuff of his sweater. I observed characteristics such as these, brought on by the disease itself or by the countless medications and treatments intended to battle the leukemia. I also noted, of course, the things that made Grandpa Grandpa--and those things remained despite, or perhaps in spite of, the disease. I was ever amazed by Grandpa's ability to present such power and control while remaining so openly laid back and accepting of whatever was placed before him.

I saw, too, those physical characteristics that defined Grandpa. Grandpa's blue eyes were framed by a pair of basic bifocals above which was a pair of Irish eyebrows. I don't even know exactly what Irish eyebrows are, nor if there exists such a thing outside of my own mind, but somehow I have always thought that Grandpa had very Irish eyebrows. The mouth was one of Grandpa's most defining characteristics; his bottom lip, originating somewhere out of sight, beyond the mouth's opening, flowed out and rolled over, like a wave cresting in the Atlantic. His ears, long and large, were created to take in all that was happening around him, I was sure. Grandpa's hair, eternally a dark, dark brown, appearing black in most light, presented a silent argument against his years. And then there were the Rockport shoes. I know, shoes are shoes, but not to Grandpa. Grandpa would wear nothing on his feet other than Rockport shoes. Oddly, but truthfully, the shoes defined Grandpa as well.

Grandpa placed his glass gently on the small, round marble top of the table between us. His hand, now free, began tapping out a beat on his knee while we listened to Duke Ellington's orchestra play in the distant background. The sounds of meshing words and laughter, each voice fighting to be heard above the next, virtually drowned Mr. Ellington and his band. But like I said, those ears were something special. They heard the music when no one else could. When I saw the fingers dancing and then the Rockports tapping, all my reservations and fears melted away and I was sitting with Grandpa, just like always, not with Grandpa's leukemia. Warm, welcomed, and wanted, I felt not only safe in his presence, but also important, as his love was unconditional and unmistakable.

That Christmas, as we sat there, Grandpa told me how proud he was of me, how handsome I had become. I had always, since I could remember, felt Grandpa's pride; I never, however, heard him say the words. They were wonderful, magical words to an eighteen-year-old who just graduated at the bottom of his class and who couldn't seem to find his place. Those words meant more to me than anything. We continued to sit and talk. It didn't matter what we talked about, whether it was his days playing piano with the orchestra or what Grandma was fixing in the kitchen.

Grandpa retold my favorite story of his time in the war. When he received bundles of letters or packages tied with string, each string was carefully untied, never cut, and placed in his pocket among the many others that had accumulated over time. When things became too much to bear, when his thoughts became his enemies, or when he found himself crouched in a foxhole for extended periods of time, he would reach into his pocket and pull out his strings. The same strings that were so carefully untied and removed from their boxes and bundles were now a tangled, knotty mess. Perfect. Having little control over anything else, Grandpa would then proceed to untangle his strings, restoring order and sense, protecting his mind from that which was weighing heavy and helping to pass the time. I always thought of that pocket tumbleweed as Grandpa's friend--a very good, if unlikely, friend having helped him through many hard times.

Our conversations would continue until Grandma called us all to dinner. Small clubs emerged from all corners of the house to meet at the dining table where all became one, big club, the most important club of all. After a brief confusion over who should sit where and who was to have what to drink, we would settle in for the feast. All disorganization seemed to disappear. Men stopped laughing, glasses stopped clinking, women stopped serving and cousins stopped giggling. Everyone bowed their heads for the blessing. I waited for a moment, and then slowly raised my own head, only slightly. Careful to keep my right eye squeezed shut, I opened my left eye, glanced around at the family that shared the table and tried to understand, to accept that this was my family, that I was - am a part of all this. I turned to look at Grandpa. Reflections of the candle flames danced in the lenses of his bifocals hiding his eyes, though I was sure they were closed. A halo of pride glowed brilliantly around him and Grandpa said the blessing. Grandpa said the blessing and Grandma cried and all was right with the world.

Chapter II

"Hey, kid, get us some more bread over here, willya?" I nodded and obediently went to the kitchen to get the creep some more bread. I felt my temperature rising beneath my little black "yessir" vest and when I returned to the creep's table, bread in hand, it was all I could do to keep from telling this guy what he could do with the bread. I imagined myself doing just that and suddenly I was playing a bit part in a bad mob picture.

Paulie "The Creep", without so much as removing the white linen napkin that was tucked into his collar, stood up, knocking his chair over backward, pulled a large automatic weapon from beneath the table and proceeded to spray the restaurant with gunfire....

"Hey, whassamatta witch you, kid? You gonna give me dat bread or you gonna stand there witchyer pie hole open?" I opted to give him the bread. Man, I had to get out of there.

At about ten o'clock pm, the manager of the restaurant approached me. She stopped in front of me, signature cigarette in hand. Looking more like a smoking pencil, the cigarette teetered between her knotted knuckles. She raised her twisted fingers to her mouth. Her lips wrapped around the filtered end, in slow motion, her cheeks caved in, and the coal at the tip glowed intensely while she drew a deep pull of smoke from her skinny friend. I could see her entire body fill up with smoke. She released the cigarette from her lips' grasp and with smoke rolling out of every opening in her face, she growled, "Honey, you can go."

After changing into street clothes, I walked up the hill toward the local billiards hall. The December air bit my cheeks and I bumped the tempo up a notch. During the short walk, so many thoughts battled for space in my head that no single one lasted long enough to be identified before being pushed out by the next. Before long, I had reached my destination. I knew this based not only on the sight of the little oasis in the middle of this tundra, but also on the warmth that was growing within me, the hastened rhythm of my heartbeat.

I pulled open the door and the sounds of the jukebox tried to escape. I quickly stepped inside and pulled the door shut behind me. Heads nodded as I walked by and I found my way to a table in the corner of the hall where several of my friends were shooting a game of pool.

"Hey, man! Sit down, have a beer." I, being underage, opted for a root beer, but nonetheless I obeyed, sitting down on the edge of a chair without even removing my coat, without even thinking about it, actually.

"I tried to call you earlier, there was no answer."

"Yeah, I just got out of work and my folks are out of town. My grandpa is in the hospital again," I explained.

"Really? Sorry to hear that, man."

"Don't worry about it, he'll be fine. He's been in and out of that place since he was diagnosed and that was over a year ago." I lifted the frosted mug left by the waitress to my lips and drank its contents. I welcomed the flavor as it woke my tongue. The flow bit my throat as the brisk air had nipped my cheeks only minutes before.

As I set the empty glass on the table, a strange feeling saturated my being and I stood up so abruptly that I knocked my chair over with the backs of my knees, just like Paulie "The Creep". I had to call home. I had to talk to my sister. I fumbled painfully for a quarter in my pockets, my hands still frozen from the walk. I pushed the coin into the slot and punched the numbers.

"Hello?" My little sister answered on the second ring.

"Hey, it's me. What's up?"

"I thought you were supposed to come straight home from work."

"Yeah, well, I'm on my way. Is everything all right?"

"Yeah, I guess. Mom is at the hospital with Grandpa and Dad is on his way there now."

"Okay. See you in a few."

"Okay, bye."

"Bye."

I returned the receiver to its cradle and drew a deep breath. I stood for a moment with my hand on the receiver, aware of my lungs swelling with the stale air of the bar. Without a single word to anyone, I left. I sprinted all the way home, partly in an effort to keep warm, partly because of something else. Something else that I couldn't quite place my finger on. When I got home, I found a degree of relief in simply being there, in the soothing quality of home. I sat with my sister and watched a little TV. I didn't tell her about my experience at the local billiards hall or the sense of near panic I felt as I ran home. It no longer seemed important. The warm coziness of the couch swallowed me, and the last thing I saw before my eyelids surrendered to the hypnotizing flashes of light from the television was my little sister. She smiled at me as I faded away.

◆

"**NO!!**" The scream ripped through the early morning silence. I could actually feel the sound waves bounce against my face. "IT'S NOT TRUE! NO!" Terror gave way to desperation and the cries grew quieter, haunting me as I sat up in bed, heart pounding. Surely, my heart was protruding from my chest with each beat the way I had seen so many times on Saturday morning TV. With a gentle knock, my father slowly opened the door. The sobs from my little sister's bedroom down the hall sounded louder, there now being a clear path from her room to mine uninterrupted by closed doors. My father crossed the room, his dark silhouette against the rectangular light of the doorway growing larger as he approached. He sat on the edge of my bed and as my eyes adjusted to the unwelcome light that was now streaming into the room, he faded into existence like a ghost making himself visible to me. I saw the pain in his face. No one had taught him how to do what he was now doing.

"Grandpa died last night", he said. "I'm so sorry." Somehow, the first half of the sentence escaped me temporarily and those last three words rang in my ears.

I was in the fifth grade at the time and all of my so-called friends had decided to cross me off the friend list, offering no explanation. No one spoke to me anymore. Stares and giggles were directed at me. I would pretend to be sick, hoping to avoid the nightmare that awaited me at school each day. I crawled into myself because I had nowhere else to go. I allowed access to no one. After all, those formerly allowed access now laughed at me. One weekend morning, as I was heading out the front door with no destination other than away from all living souls, my father called out to stop me. I turned around slowly in response, wishing he would go away. He looked at me for a moment and, saying nothing, wrapped his arms around me and squeezed so tightly and unexpectedly that I lost my breath for a moment. I never felt such conflicting emotion, as I stood there lifeless in my father's arms. I wanted to accept his love; I wanted to squeeze him back. Never in my life had I wanted anything more than to allow my daddy to protect me...but I couldn't. I could allow access to no one. I felt my father's pain, and he felt mine. "I'm so sorry," he whispered. As I backed away from the embrace, I became aware that my father's eyes were capable of producing tears. I closed the door softly behind me, took a breath of the fresh outdoor air, and I walked.

"What?" I said.

"Grandpa died," he repeated. I heard the words my father had just said and, as I took them in, I tried to stay focused, recognizing the importance of the subject at hand.

"Are you okay?" I heard my father say.

"I guess," I returned, and then I simply sat there. Nodding toward the hallway, I asked, "Is she okay?"

"Maybe you should go and see, maybe try to comfort her some." I walked down the hallway wondering what I would say when I got to my sister's room. I couldn't come up with a single thing and so I just sat on the bed beside her and listened to her cry. I wished that I would cry too. I tried to make the tears come, but they refused. I must be an awful person. I felt nothing.

Further supporting the awful person theory, I used my grandfather's death as a cowardly escape. I called the restaurant and told them I needed a couple of days. I never went back.

I was asked to be a pallbearer at Grandpa's funeral. I had only one suit, so I pulled it out of the closet and, upon fastening the pants, realized that they were at least two inches too short. A fitting preface to the longest day of my life. I spent the entire day convinced that Grandma was angry with me, though now I can recall nothing to offer justification for such an absurd idea. I knew this then as well as I know it now, but it changed neither the reality nor the intensity of the feeling. I was sure that each time she looked in my direction, she did so through veils of disappointment. I wondered if she would ever forgive me and then I wondered what on earth she would be forgiving me for. The guilt was suffocating me. I watched as well wishers spoke to me and shook my hand. But where was I? Looking down on the scene from far far away. I wondered if perhaps my secret wish had been granted and I was watching this world from my pseudo-reality within the shiny glass Christmas ball. Suddenly it was as if somebody had clapped their hands over my ears like the professional wrestlers did on television. "POP!" Like the sound of my Christmas ball breaking open, there I was. I swallowed hard. Through the ringing in my ears, I heard the voices of the well wishers once again. Whirlpools of hot blood swirled behind my face. Man, I had to get out of there.

I excused myself and walked down the hall to a lounge area, a small rectangle of a room. The walls were lined with chairs: most of them comfy living room-style arm chairs, a few the folding kind with the name of the funeral home stenciled on the back--the kind my father would borrow each Thanksgiving to accommodate the large number of dinner guests, the kind that inevitably surrounded the kids' table. Beside a few of the comfy chairs occupying the corners of the room, stood a polished, dark wood table upon which sat an ashtray and a lamp. Hanging on the walls were paintings of the type one might check out of the local library when expecting important dinner guests, the kind that fooled no one. I briefly considered the motive for hanging such "art" and then noticed a coffee urn brewing on a table against the wall. The familiar therapeutic value of the cup in hand beckoned and the stack of Styrofoam cups towered beside the urn suddenly took precedence over concern for the interior decorating style or lack thereof. I helped myself to one of the cups, held it beneath the spigot, and pushed on the handle for a welcome rush of hot, caffeinated security.

I chose one of the living room style armchairs and, careful not to spill my self-control, sat down. My pants, already two inches too short, rose even higher exposing my thin black socks as they bunched around my ankles. Stan Laurel came to mind. My bunched up socks made me think of sock garters, which made me think of Stan Laurel. This made me smile, if only for the sheer ridiculousness of having had the thought at all. I wondered if Grandpa wore sock garters.

So there I sat in the funeral home waiting room. I wondered what people in a funeral home might be waiting for. I looked around and discovered that, for the first time that day, I was alone. Apparently people in a funeral home had nothing to wait for. So what was I waiting for? Maybe I was waiting for Grandma to find me and offer forgiveness. Maybe I was waiting for the day to end so I could get out of these pants. Maybe I was waiting to simply feel. But this waiting room was different. No one ever came to fetch me. No one ever called my name and said, "Come on back," which would be my cue to toss the old magazine with the mailing label carefully cut out onto the table and vacate my chair. In fact, there weren't even any old magazines. This waiting room was very different. I just sat and waited and waited.

Chapter III

The next Christmas came just as it did each year. The sounds were there, the smells were there, the clubs continued to meet, and the aunts and mommies were making a fuss over Grandma's nativity scene. Everything was the same, but everything was different.

I got a soda in a short plastic cup, walked into the living room, placed my cup on the white and gray marble that capped the table beside the chair, grasped each pant leg just above the knee, gave a little tug, and settled into the chair. I observed the family from just outside the Christmas playing field. I felt angry that I sat alone, wished that someone would come to sit with me at the sidelines. I wished this not because I desired the company, the compassion, but rather because I became screamingly aware that I was still waiting. And I was still the only one waiting. I realized then that the waiting was not in the funeral home lounge at all.

The wait was in me. I picked up my cup and rubbed it gently as I sat, as if a genie would appear and offer me contentment, if not the ability to feel that I continued to wait for. The genie never appeared. I closed my eyes. I listened hard. Mr. Ellington's orchestra remained silent. If only I had Grandpa's ears. I sat there until Grandma called everyone to the dining room. Everyone gathered around the table and I joined them. Once it was decided who would sit where and who would have what to drink, we all settled into our seats and bowed our heads for the blessing. There was a brief silence, the loudest I've ever known, and Grandma cried. As if not to be outdone, aunts and mommies joined in, and so it went.

The year, most of the time, went like any other, with ups and downs and ins and outs. I can't recall any significant time being spent thinking consciously about Grandpa, though thoughts did occur. These thoughts, usually, were not welcomed but resented. I felt angry and guilty and although I did not know why this was so, it was so and I was powerless--a characteristic I had grown quite familiar with. That year I spent a lot of time in my shiny glass Christmas ball, aware of little outside of myself. I felt out of touch with my family and friends and spent much time pressing my face against the glass ball, peering out, observing life rather than living it. At times I found myself wondering if I was alive at all anymore. After all, is there such a thing, I would ask myself, as alive in the absence of living? I don't mean to suggest that when Grandpa died, I died with him, though I believe a small part of me did. To consider his leaving this world, however, and my feelings surrounding his death, was to place my own life beneath the magnifying glass, revealing where I was or where I was not in my life. Simply put, I was confused. I was confused and Grandpa was something that made one small corner of my world less confusing. Nothing ironed out the wrinkles of my life like a little Duke Ellington and a good story. With Grandpa gone and the music silent, who was to alleviate the confusion?

Grandpa always came home to the music. I
waited.

Chapter IV

I was working for a small roofing and siding company that focused its efforts on the poorer sections of the city. Inevitably, on any given day, at least half a dozen unemployed men would approach the boss looking for work. Today was no exception. I watched from my post atop the ladder as the boss turned down each plea, seemingly without a thought. I felt bad for the men and wondered, as they headed for the next jobsite, what their lives were like, who their families were. The thought that those men existed outside of the brief moment in which their paths happened to cross with mine was somehow reassuring. As I fumbled to hold a nail in place with my bulky winter gloves, ultimately watching it fall to the ground below, I noticed a man walking down the broken sidewalk toward the boss. This man was large, about six feet tall and very solid, his dark brown skin made darker by the shadow cast on his face by the brim of his cap. Even from this distance, I noted the big hands that seemed to dictate the power within this man. His short, cropped, snow-white beard interrupted the blackness of his face and something about him made me warm on this cold December day. As he approached the boss, I cringed. Unable to watch the boss trample this man's self-esteem, sending him back to his family jobless at Christmastime, I forced myself to return to work. I struggled to retrieve a nail with my marshmallow fingers from the pouch at my hip. Just as the frustration began to mount, the boss yelled up at me. "Come on down here a minute!" Amazed to see the big, dark man still standing beside the boss, and further amazed by the brilliant white smile he wore on his face, I scrambled down the ladder to the driveway below.

"This is James, he's going to be working with us on this job."

"How ya doin', Eric?" He extended his large hand to take mine.

"How'd you know my name?"

"Uh... the boss told me," he laughed.

I felt silly for getting wrapped up in the warmth he radiated and asking such a ridiculous question. "Oh, yeah," I laughed through my embarrassment, "I'm good, thanks, how are you?" "

Doin' fine, doin' fine." He said in his deep gravelly voice.

"Okay," the boss interjected, "I want you to take James around to the back and show him what we got here. Then you two can get started and work your way around the house from there. I'll continue here in the front."

"Okay," I said.

"Thanks again, boss," James said. "Just don't make me sorry," the boss returned in his ultra-warm manner. And off to work we went. So there we were, big James and myself standing in the backyard of this house, a blanket of snow trying desperately to camouflage the garbage that littered the landscape. We both stood silent for a moment while we looked up at the backside of the house and contemplated the work that lay before us. I always took a minute or two to ponder the job ahead. I was sure that James, standing beside me, was pondering the job ahead of him as well.

I must admit, initially, though I liked James, I felt a little bit violated. After all, I worked most often alone. I enjoyed the quiet, the think-time it offered, provided my thoughts didn't spin out of control as they seemed to do at times. I wasn't sure I was ready to share my space with someone new. What if James was a talker? Worse yet, what if he expected me to be a talker? Perhaps it would have been better if the boss hadn't had this temporary lapse in character that resulted in my having a new partner to pollute my perceived solitude. I guiltily pushed that idea out of my head and did my best to move forward with an open mind.

I showed James around our little corner of the work site and informed him of where to find tools that he would need. James was very receptive and before long, we were ready to get started. We began tearing off the existing siding boards, rotten with age, and tossing them aside as we went. We worked until lunchtime before I realized that neither of us had spoken so much as a single word since the removal of the first board. It was as if James knew how I felt about my friend, Silence, and chose to allow my friend and I to become better acquainted with the idea before becoming better acquainted with the man. Lunch, as well as the remainder of the workday went much the same way the morning had, each of us choosing to work in respectful silence.

"Clean up!" I heard the boss yell from the house somewhere. I glanced at the time and sure enough, it was four-thirty in the afternoon. I could set my watch to the boss's bellow. He wanted to be certain that we were packed up and off the jobsite no later than five o'clock.

"Eric, I've gotta run some errands on the other side of town tonight so I won't be able to take you to the bus." Usually, the boss would drop me off at the bus stop where I would catch the chariot to my suburban life.

"I'll get you there, man," James offered. "I have my truck, it'd be my pleasure."

"Truck, huh?" I challenged. "So why did you walk here this morning? If you remember, James," I teased, "You arrived via sidewalk."

"Look, boy, you want a ride or you want to bust my chops?"

"All right, all right, I appreciate it." He pointed toward an old Ford pickup truck that sat at the curb directly in front of the house.

"There she is," James said, "Hop in!" I looked at the truck, I looked back at James. That truck wasn't here a minute ago, I thought to myself. "It's been a long day," I sighed. I shook my head and laughed it off. "Okay, Jeeves, let's go home."

"Oh, Jeeves, now is it? You best watch yourself, boy," James scolded. I pulled the door open, climbed in, and pulled it shut behind me. As promised, James delivered me to the bus stop and drove on, leaving me to wait for my suburban-bound chariot. On the ride home, I thought about James. I thought about the truck, and then oddly my thoughts turned to Grandpa. It wasn't necessarily the thoughts themselves that I found to be odd, but the absence of discomfort and resentment. These thoughts were welcomed. I smiled. I leaned my head against the window. I felt my teeth vibrate and my lips tickle with the rhythm of the bus and I smiled again.

A few minutes later, I opened my eyes and saw my stop approaching. I pulled the cord to signal the driver, hung my tool belt on my shoulder, and prepared to re-enter suburbia. I stepped off the bus and looked around. How amazing it was that only a few minutes previous, I would have sworn I was in another world. A strange mixture of gratitude and shame left me as quickly as it came and I walked down the unbroken sidewalk toward home. As usual, thoughts filled my head as I watched the square sections of neatly combed concrete pass below my feet. I was fully aware of the existence of this tangle of thoughts, though, curiously unaware of any thought in particular or of any significance it may or may not carry. I didn't raise my head until I was directly across the street from my house, as if my subconscious mind had counted the sections of sidewalk and knew precisely how many bridged the distance from the bus stop to my house.

Yep, that's my house, the same one that everyone always said was so huge, so perfect. "Your folks must be loaded," kids would say to me as I was growing up in this house. "You guys are like the perfect family living in the perfect house." Well, they were half right anyway. My eyes scanned the perfect landscaping that my father spent endless hours maintaining, the newly painted shutters, even a disgustingly cute, furry little squirrel skipping across the front lawn. I half expected Snow White to round the corner singing some honey-drenched song while birds flitted about her head. If there were any imperfections at all, they were undoubtedly attributable to yours truly, a result of a grossly indifferent lawn mowing session. Luckily, I thought, the snow is covering the lawn for awhile--one less testimony to my incompetence. I cussed at the squirrel and crossed the road toward the house.

◆

I jerked awake, instinctively my right arm extended from beneath the covers and pounded the snooze button in search of another nine minutes of silence. Whoever thought up the nine-minute concept anyway? Why not just make it ten? Anyway, no deal. Any chance I may have had for a couple more winks went south when I decided to analyze the eternal question of the alarm clock snooze. I considered, only half-seriously, taking a shower. Deciding against it, rather than admitting to an extreme lack of motivation, I reasoned that I would just be dirty again in an hour. I pulled on the same jeans I wore the day previous, pulled on a ratty blue stocking cap, more to camouflage my bed head than to keep it warm, grabbed my tool belt, and I was out the door.

As I watched the concrete squares, I thought about the monotony that had become my life: same thing, day in and day out, with nothing to show for any of it. I stopped in at the convenience store and turned around to check the clock above the door: 7:07 am. Three minutes before my chariot arrives. I nodded at the man behind the counter, decided that he resembled a clown in his multi-colored uniform shirt, and wondered if he knew how stupid he looked. When I arrived at the coffee station and poured myself a tall cup, it smelled like it had been on that burner for a week. But I paid Bozo and crossed the street to meet the bus. I stood at the curb waiting, lifted the Styrofoam cup to my mouth, and blew into the little rectangular hole in the plastic lid in a lame attempt to cool the contents. I slowly tipped the cup back until the liquid touched my lip. I quickly realized, as I ran my tongue over my lips to make sure that they were still there, that this coffee was much too hot for human consumption. The bus pulled up and the doors squeaked open. The driver took one look at the Styrofoam cup in my hand and shook his head, pointing at the "No Food or Drink" sign posted above his head. Well, that's about right, I thought. I gingerly set the cup down on the curb, as if having taken the care to do so freed me of any litterbug status. I climbed the steps, dropped my change in the coin box, and found a seat.

Upon exiting the bus, I saw the boss waiting in the company truck across the street. I glanced for oncoming traffic and bolted across to the truck.

"Mornin'," the boss said as I hoisted myself into the passenger seat.

"Yeah, I suppose it is."

"James is gonna meet us at the jobsite."

"Okay."

Five minutes later, five silent minutes had it not been for the rumble of the diesel engine, we arrived at the jobsite. James was sitting on the front step of the house as we pulled up to the curb. We exited the truck and walked toward the back to unload the tools.

"Mornin', James," I managed.

"Ah, yessir, it certainly is a beautiful world we live in, ain't it, Mr. Eric?"

"To be honest, James, I hadn't noticed."

"You'll see, boy." The gravelly laugh escaped him as he stood up and arched his back. He turned and walked toward the back of the house. "Heh, heh, yes, Lord, he'll see." I shook my head and looked at the boss. He just shrugged and motioned for my help with the unloading.

I guess we had been working a good couple of hours before James broke the silence with a startling, "So..." Without so much as a glance in his direction, "So," I parroted.

"What are you about, boy?"

"What am I about?" I asked, confused by the question.

"Mm-hmm," James grunted. "What color is your Kool-Aid? What makes your clock tick?"

I couldn't believe that someone had just asked me about the color of my Kool-Aid. "You're lookin' at it, James; this is what I do."

I wished we could go back to being silent coworkers. I continued pounding nails. For a little while James continued gabbing, though I didn't hear the actual words that spilled mercilessly from his mouth. I think he eventually took the hint and the talking ceased though the broad smile never abandoned his face. I wondered what went on inside this man that he could appear to always be so happy. And though I wouldn't admit it, I envied that man. James hummed and grinned and pounded nails. I just pounded nails. Without the distraction of James' inquiries, I began to feel as if I was

turning inside out. My thoughts, having swallowed my brain, had nowhere else to go within, and thus turned without, my entire existence becoming that which only moments before merely dusted the lonely corners of my mind.

I felt my throat slowly closing, my breaths becoming shallow. The fact that this was a normal occurrence for me made the experience no less terrifying. The sound of my racing heart echoed in my head, threatening to drown out the cheerful humming that still fought to be heard somewhere in the distance. The sporadic puffs that escaped my lungs forming clouds as they met with the cold air ceased to exist. I couldn't breath. I was sure I was going to die, just as sure as I was each time previous. I swore my throat had completely closed at this point and I squeezed my eyes shut. Suddenly, I was thinking about brussel sprouts. Mom would make me eat at least two of the five contaminating my plate before I could be excused from the table. I would chew them cautiously and try to swallow, but my swallow reflex wouldn't respond to the little green balls. So, I would chew some more and try again and again.

The humming, somewhere a million miles away, slowly grew louder. I tried to focus on the melody while I waited for my swallower to kick in. The pounding of my heart weakened to a whisper and my swallow reflex began functioning as my throat slowly opened. I drew a deep breath. I turned to look at James, smiling and humming and swinging away with his hammer. I smiled and acknowledged, if only to myself, that that big, curious, happy man brought me back. James glanced over in my direction, nodded, and continued working. As the day went on, I thought again about James's seemingly eternal happy state. I remembered sitting across from a therapist when I was seventeen and explaining to him how I felt.

"I see everyone around me as having a base level of happiness. It seems that folks are generally happy and factors can periodically interrupt that base level and cause one to feel temporarily angry or sad, but once the intruding factor has vacated or been dealt with, they return to their base level of happiness. Does that make sense?"

"It doesn't matter whether it makes sense to me," he offered in his best shrink voice. *"What matters is where you see yourself fitting into this theory. Where is your base level?"*

"Well, I feel like I have this base level of indifference, I guess, and I need the intruding factors to interrupt that in order to feel happy, you know? And when that factor has subsided, I, too return to my base level, only my base level is that indifference. It's like this emotional ladder and I've always been a few rungs below everyone else."

I stopped what I was doing for a moment and looked at James smiling away. I noticed that he stood exactly three rungs higher than me on his ladder. I had to laugh at the absurdity; it was too perfect.

"James?"

"Lord, the boy speaks." James turned toward me, "What is it, boy?"

"Never mind."

"Ah, yes. Never mind. I'm glad you brought that up."

"What?"

"Boy, you never pay me no mind."

"Ah, I get it. Never mind. Clever, James."

"Thank you, but I ain't shootin' for clever."

"Just what are you shootin' for James? Please enlighten me because I just can't figure you out."

"You can't figure me out? Boy, I am what I am. It's you that takes the figurin'."

"What the hell are you talking about, James?! I am what I am too! What else would I be?!"

"You tell me, boy," James said calmly.

"I am what I am. I just told you that." I was getting angry. I never should have opened my mouth.

"And what is it that you are?" The calmer James sounded, the angrier I got and he still had that damn grin on his face. Man, I was beginning to really dislike this guy.

"I don't know, James, okay? Just forget I ever said anything." I turned back to my work and took a deep breath. Man, I wanted to get out of there. Several silent minutes passed since our stimulating conversation when suddenly, once again, James broke the silence.

"Anyway you already know."

"Know what?" I asked, not sure I even wanted an answer.

"The answer," James returned matter-of-factly.

"Here we go again." I sighed, "The answer to what, James?"

"The answer to what you were going to ask me," James said, never looking away from his work. "You want to know why you're standing down there?"

"Down where?"

"On that ladder. Look, boy, do you want help or do you want to go for round two?" He couldn't be talking about my "emotional ladder" theory, could he? I thought. Of course he couldn't. How could he know? It was just a coincidence. I'm sure he was just talking about how he got ahead of me as the "new guy" on the job. Then there is the issue of this phantom Ford truck that seemed to appear out of nowhere. There is a perfectly reasonable explanation: I am a fruit loop. The remainder of the day crawled by without words. I felt a little guilty about the way I spoke to James earlier. After all, he really didn't do anything wrong, right? It's me who is apparently losing my marbles. But despite the guilt and semi-remorse, I said nothing. "Clean up!"

I lay in bed that night, staring at the ceiling. I thought again about my ladder and what James had said. I wished I had someone to talk to. I thought of the talks that Grandpa and I used to have. I wish you were here, Grandpa, I thought. I glanced around the darkness of my room wondering for a moment if I had just said that out loud. I laid still for a moment listening to the silence. Ah, why not, I thought.

"Grandpa," I said out loud, "I need you. I don't know what to do." I felt an odd, unexpected relief in saying those words and I proceeded to tell Grandpa how I was feeling. I cried as I spoke. Physically and emotionally exhausted, I eventually fell asleep on my tear-soaked pillow.

The alarm screamed. I pounded the clock, once again begging the snooze gods for nine minutes of mercy. My plea was granted, and keeping up my end of the bargain, I slid out of bed on the tenth minute. I climbed into the shower and stood under a steady stream of hot water. As it drooled over my face, I closed my eyes. I covered my ears with my hands and imagined I was in a forest somewhere in a rainstorm. I stood there for twenty minutes before I surrendered to the fact that all the soap and water in the world, rainstorm or not, won't wash away tired. So I got dressed, grabbed my tool belt, and I was out the door.

I arrived at the jobsite that morning, same as always, with the boss.

"Good mornin', gentlemen!" James called as he struggled to his feet and arched his back.

"Mornin', James," the boss and I returned, in stereo. The three of us unloaded the truck to the tune of James's humming. As usual, James and I took our places at the backside of the house and set up our ladders. We got right to work and James got right to interfering with my peace and quiet.

"Have a good night, did ya?" He asked cheerily.

"I guess, yeah."

"Slept okay then?"

I guess." I stopped working for a moment, looking at my feet as if they offered some clue as to what my mind was searching for. "You know, now that you mention it, I think I had a dream or somethin' last night."

"That right? A dream?" the happy man inquired.

"Yeah," I responded looking to my feet for details.

"Well, what about, boy?"

"My grandpa. I wonder where that came from." I answered thoughtfully.

"Must be in your heart, boy," James offered, "Lotta folks seem to think that dreams come from your head; well, I know otherwise."

"You sayin' that dreams come from the heart?" I asked.

"That's exactly what I'm sayin', boy. Dreams are a funny thing but they ain't all that folks try to make them out to be. Alls I'm sayin' is that you must have the man in your heart if you're havin' dreams about him, dig?"

"James, if it's all the same to you, I'd rather not talk about it right now."

"Suit yourself, boy," James said, "But you should know, you done the right thing."

"What do you mean, the right thing?" I asked.

"Inviting your granddaddy back into your heart," he responded, "I told you that you knew the answer, now hand me some of them nails, boy, I've got a lotta work to do here." I reached into the nail pouch hanging from my tool belt and grabbed a handful of nails. I extended my arm toward the ladder that James was standing on, two rungs above where I stood on my own ladder.

"Yeah," I said, "Maybe I did."

It was quiet that day, still. It wasn't just the lack of conversation, it was the air. I don't know, it was something, I just couldn't quite place it. As was usually the case, when the world is quiet around me, my mind makes its presence known. I thought about sitting around the dinner table with my family: my two sisters, my parents, and me. We always ate dinner together; that was the rule. I can remember numerous occasions when my father would remind my sisters and me, "You know, your grandparents are getting old. They may not be with us much longer." "Shut up, Dad," my older sister would fire at him, "That's a real nice thing to say!" My little sister saw the opportunity in the little controversy that was brewing at the table. While my older sister attacked, and my father defended his intended point, my little sister somehow vanished, long gone before anyone took notice of the empty chair that sat behind her plate, virtually untouched but for the slight rearrangement of a few peas. I smiled slightly as I thought of my little sister's mastery of the art of dinner table escape.

My smile faded as I thought about the truth of what my father had said. My mother and father always encouraged us to write our grandparents, to visit them, to let them know how much we love them. I don't think I ever wrote a letter to any of my grandparents. And when I reached an age at which my parents would offer me the choice, more often than not, I opted not to visit either. My father was right. Contrary to what I wanted to believe as a child, as a grandchild, grandparents don't simply stay. One day, grandparents die, just like regular folks. So now Grandpa was dead and I wasn't there to say goodbye. That was today's reality. I thought about my conversation with James earlier and what he had said about inviting Grandpa back into my heart.

"James?"

"Mm-hmm?"

"Nothing," I said, feeling my muscles tighten and my toes curling up inside my work boots. I wasn't ready.

"It's okay, boy. I understand." And I believe he did. We quietly returned to our respective tasks and the day remained quiet, not even the hum of that big, happy man to disturb its stillness.

Chapter V

"Grandpa?" I inquired of the darkness, "Am I crazy? I mean, here I am, lying in bed talking to nothing. Am I talking to nothing?" I hesitated briefly. "You're there, aren't you? I'm sorry, Grandpa. I wanted to say goodbye." I wondered if the intense emotion I was feeling was a result of self-pity or of genuine sadness and sorrow. "I always question myself, Grandpa. Why is it that I am never able to trust my own thoughts, my own feelings?" I lied quiet and still for several minutes. For the first time since, well, since I could remember, the stillness did not set the mind's stage for the circus of thoughts that over the years had become synonymous with quiet. On the contrary, my mind was as quiet and still as the room around me. I felt so relaxed and became suddenly aware of how completely exhausted I was. I moved around in my bed, my legs seeking the freshest, coolest spot in the sheets and I nestled my head into my pillow. "Goodnight, Grandpa."

I saw the reflection of the American flag waving in the glass. I slowly pulled the door open and stepped inside. I looked around, eyes scanning the oil portraits that decorated the walls. Priests and nuns stared back at me from beyond the polished wooden frames in which they resided. I walked cautiously and purposefully down the hall. I didn't recognize the context that I suddenly existed in, though it felt familiar somehow. I felt like I knew this place, I just didn't recognize it visually. I continued down the turquoise Berber carpeted floor. A photograph hung on the wall to my left. I approached it and looked carefully. "I know these people," I whispered. It was my fifth grade class picture. I realized why this place felt familiar to me. It was the Catholic school I had attended as a boy. Yes, it didn't look the same, but there was no mistaking this feeling. I stood in the hallway at St. Joseph's Elementary School. As I examined the photo, I found myself remembering the hell they called fifth grade. I was so alone then. What did I ever do to those kids that they turned on me the way they did? I was so alone. "Who am I kidding?" I said out loud, "I'm still alone." I squeezed my eyes shut and tightened my fists. I took a deep breath and walked on. I came to a set of four steps leading to another long hallway and proceeded up the stairs dragging my fingers along the worn wooden railing as I went. My arm quickly and instinctively retracted when the railing thrust a splinter into my left forefinger. I decided that my hands would be safer in my pockets and it was there, in my right pants pocket, that I felt something. I pulled it out to investigate. It was an envelope. On the front, in my own handwriting, it said simply: Grandpa. I tore open the envelope to inspect its contents and found a letter. I unfolded the paper to reveal a very brief note:

Dear Grandpa,
I love you. I need you.
Love,
Eric

I folded the letter and put it back into the envelope.

"Whatchya got there?" The voice came from nowhere.

"Grandpa?"

"Yo?" I couldn't believe it. I lifted my head and there, standing about thirty feet down the pale yellow painted cinderblock hallway, stood my grandpa.

"Grandpa?" I said again, unable to contain my disbelief.

"It's me," he said. I walked toward him now. My short steps slowly stole the distance between us until I stood immediately before him. I looked at his eyes. Oh my God, I thought, it really is Grandpa. I threw my arms around him and felt his breath against my cheek as we embraced, his strong hands on my back.

This was real, but how? I stood back to look again at my grandpa.

"I don't understand, Grandpa," I said through my tears.

"Why are you here? How?"

"You needed me," he responded. "I'm here to help."

"But you are here now, can't you stay?" I pleaded.

"I was allowed to come back in order to do this job," he said as he gripped my shoulder and looked into my eyes. "I came to help, not to stay." Grandpa's face began to blur as my eyes welled up with tears. It was like looking at a reflection in a pond having been interrupted by the eternal ripples caused by a tossed stone.

"I understand," I managed, trying my best to mean what I said.

"You have nothing to feel guilty about, Eric," Grandpa told me, "Not me, not your grandma, not your life. You have nothing to apologize for." I just stood and listened, listened and cried. "You are a good boy and I am proud of you," he continued. "You have to remember to allow your feelings to be your feelings. You are a passionate and sensitive young man. Accept this as a blessing, Eric, not as a curse. If you have a feeling, if you entertain a thought, it is real. Trust it."

"But, I feel too much," I cried. "My thoughts swallow me, Grandpa."

"No. It's you that swallows you," Grandpa countered. "You try so hard to make sense out of each thought, to analyze every feeling as it surfaces. This is what clutters your mind. Allow your thoughts to happen, you don't need to take inventory."

"I'll try," I said.

"Hey," he said, "Remember my tangle of string?"

I smiled. It was a comforting thought. "I remember."

"Well, I started that whole thing because I didn't want my thoughts to take over," he explained. "Better to have a tangled mess of string in your pocket than a tangled mess of thoughts in your noodle." I laughed. It felt good.

"Untangling those strings when times got tough was my way to keep from attempting to untangle my thoughts, which was when things really got ugly."

"Yeah," I agreed, "Only 'ugly' seems like such an understatement." Grandpa smiled at me.

"Then you understand what I'm trying to say to you?"

"Yes, I do," I replied thoughtfully. "I guess it'd be kind of hard to live life if I'm constantly second-guessing it."

"'Atta boy," Grandpa said. "If we took the time to question each note, we'd miss the music, wouldn't we?" He winked at me, so quickly I wondered if I saw it at all, and he smiled. I felt so warm, so happy, so free.

"Can you stay, please, Grandpa?"

"You know I can't." His head lowered a bit and his Irish eyebrows rose a bit. "The job is done." He smiled again. "I'm so proud of you, Eric," he said.

"Goodbye, Grandpa," I cried. Grandpa squeezed my hand and then his fingers opened slowly releasing my own. My hand fell to my side and Grandpa turned to walk away, down that long, pale yellow painted cinderblock hallway. As the distance between us grew larger and Grandpa grew smaller, I heard his voice one last time.

"You're not alone." And he was gone.

Chapter VI

The day felt different right from the start. I awoke at about six o'clock and without so much as a thought about the snooze button, I sat up in bed. I felt unusually well rested. I rubbed the dream crystals from my eyes and stretched as if I was trying to make my arms grow longer. I emerged from the tangle of sheets and headed to the bathroom. Standing in front of the mirror, one hand on each side of the sink, I leaned forward. I examined the face that examined my own. I felt a slight smile creeping across my face as I simultaneously watched the smile appear beyond the glass into which I gazed. I scrunched up my face and felt my morning stubble scrape the bottom of my nose. I stuck my tongue out and wagged it at the reflection. I laughed. We laughed. I showered quickly and got dressed. I grabbed my coat, hung my tool belt over my shoulder, and I was out the door.

I crossed the street and paused briefly, turning to look toward the house. It looked different somehow, I mean, it was the same...but somehow different. It was as if I was looking through someone else's eyes. I thought about the brainteaser that an art teacher had once shown me at St. Joe's. It was a line drawing of what appeared to me to be an old woman. The teacher encouraged me to take a different perspective, to train myself to see something different, and, with her help, eventually it became clear. The picture was indeed of an old woman; however, it was also a pretty young woman with a large hat. That pretty young woman taught me that I am in control of what I see, how I choose to perceive the world around me. If I choose to see the ugliness and sorrow in the world, it will no doubt cloud my view of the beauty and gratitude that is just as real. Somewhere along the way, I forgot that valuable lesson and here I stood, seeing my house with new eyes and re-learning one of the most important lessons of my lifetime. I cussed the cute furry little squirrel that skipped across the blanket of snow, perhaps more out of habit than anything else, and continued on.

I walked up the unbroken, neatly plowed sidewalk toward the bus stop. The square sections carried me to the corner where I stopped in at the convenience store. I nodded at Bozo as I headed for the coffee station.

"I just brewed that pot fresh, man," I heard from behind me as I pulled off my winter gloves. I thought about how the day thus far had seemed brighter and somehow felt as if I should cut the guy a break. I decided I would and turned to respond to my new friend. But that stupid shirt was screaming, "Look at me, I'm an idiot!" I turned back to the coffee station, poured a cup, pushed a plastic lid on it and carried it to the counter. I handed him my money. He smiled and nodded. I glanced up at the clock above the door: 6:47 a.m.

"Have a good one," the guy called as I headed for the door.

"If you say so," I said sarcastically without turning around. I crossed the street to the bus stop and stood on the sidewalk beside the curb. I popped the lid off the cup, hoping to cool the contents adequately before attempting consumption. I watched the morning rush hour traffic speed past and for the first time thought of that traffic not simply as speeding cars, but as people--people busy with their lives. In each car that flew by, there existed a different person with a different life, different goals, and, although they all passed me at the same point, different destinations. This thought both fascinated and comforted me. I blew gently into my cup and carefully took a small sip. The flavor was so satisfying and I could feel the trail of warmth as it traveled throughout my body. The aroma of the fresh coffee was a comfort in and of itself and I closed my eyes for a moment to focus on that comfort, savoring it. It was so nice to enjoy the moments as they unfolded, unburdened by overwhelming thoughts or feelings. Today, I simply am, I thought. It was a wonderful thought. I smiled and said to myself, "I am what I am."

The bus doors squeaked open and the driver pointed at the sign above his head. I looked into my cup. Empty. I smiled at the driver and tipped the cup until it was completely upside down. Proudly and silently claiming my personal victory, I climbed the steps, though not before respectfully placing the cup on the curb. I dropped my fare into the slot, nodded at the driver who had no concept of the satisfaction I had just experienced, and found a seat.

I arrived at the bus station downtown and found the boss parked around the corner. I opened the truck door and climbed in.

"Mornin'," I said before the boss had a chance to get a word in.

"Mornin', yerself," the boss responded. He ground the truck into gear and pulled out into the road.

"The house is comin' along pretty well, huh?" I asked.

"Uh, yeah, it looks great. We're gettin' there." He was obviously a bit taken aback by my sudden interest in communicating.

"Yeah," I continued, "Couple more days, we oughta have her knocked out." The boss never responded. We rode the rest of the way in virtual silence. I thought about the job. I thought about how run down and tired the house appeared the day we arrived on the jobsite. I thought about the work we put in removing all that was old, worn, and stressed. I thought about the care and effort we expressed while revealing the true character of the house. Witnessing the emergence of this bright, fresh, renewed house was quite a beautiful thing. We pulled up in front of the house. James stood and arched his back.

"Mornin', fellas," James said cheerily.

"Back at ya, James," I responded, finding this new energy rather amusing.

"Mornin', James," the boss said while walking to the back of the truck.

"Well, jump back," James said with a smile.

"What?" I asked. "You seem unusually sunshiny this mornin', boy."

"Yeah, I guess I am," I smiled. We unloaded the truck and took our places ready to work.

"Well, boy, tomorrow's Christmas Eve. What are you planning for the big day?"

James asked as he struggled to hold a piece of vinyl siding in place with one hand while digging in his nail pouch with the other.

"We go to my grandma and grand...well, grandma's house every Christmas," I answered awkwardly.

"I see, I see." Finally, James produced a nail from his pouch and holding it between his sausage-like fingers, he swung with the hammer. "That's nice, boy. Nothin' like family."

"Yeah," I responded, "I guess."

"You don't sound so sure about that," James taunted.

"I don't know, man. I just never feel quite right at those things, ya know? I mean, I love my family and all, I just don't fit in." I was frustrated that I wasn't able to put my feelings into words.

"Nonsense, boy," James grunted at me, never abandoning his work.

"Especially since Grandpa died," I continued, desperately wanting to make sense.

"Why is that?" James asked in such a manner that implied that he wasn't inquiring for his benefit, but for my own. He sounded like a therapist of some sort, in fact he sounded a lot like a family therapist that my parents dragged us to many years previous.

There we sat, my two sisters, my parents, and myself, all crowded together on a sofa against the wall. Across from us on a reclining roll-around leather chair was the therapist. He sat staring at me (he called it eye contact) for what seemed an eternity.

"So," he would finally say, still staring, "Tell me, Eric, what do you feel about your father?" I couldn't believe he just asked me that with my father sitting right next to me. I felt my temperature rise and though it sounds illogical to feel one's face redden, I am certain that I felt it change several shades. Meanwhile, my hands rolled into sweaty fists and I felt a prickly sensation on the back of my neck and in my armpits. I broke the so-called eye contact and shifted uncomfortably in my seat.

"He's fine," I said, glancing around the room, careful not to look at anyone.

"You look uncomfortable," the therapist said to me. "Why is that?" What, was he kidding? Of course I was uncomfortable! I looked to my feet for assistance. Nothing.

"Why don't you look at your father, Eric, and tell him how you feel." Never breaking his stare, he pulled a tissue out from the sleeve of his sweater. He trumpeted into the tissue and stuffed the disposable hanky in his crotch. This guy was a real beaut.

"I'd rather not, thanks."

"Why is that?"

"With Grandpa I never felt like I had to prove myself or laugh when I didn't find something funny. We just talked. Grandpa listened when I talked he still listens." I dropped my hands to my sides and leaned forward, lying against my ladder as I thought about how to better respond to the question of why. I couldn't come up with a good answer.

"Well, I see you have no problem explaining why you were comfortable in your granddaddy's company, boy," James pointed out, "It ain't so easy to explain why you don't feel that way with the rest of your family is it?"

"No." That was all I could think of to say at that moment.

"See, it's my theory that when there is a good reason for something, it's easy to find the words to explain it. It's when there ain't such a good reason," he continued, "that it becomes more difficult to find the words to justify, ya dig what I'm sayin', boy?" As much as I didn't want it to, what James had just said made sense.

"You, James, are somethin' else. Where'd you come from, anyway?" I laughed and shook my head. Turning to my left, I noticed that James stood only one rung above me on his ladder. "Hey," I teased, "I'm catchin' up."

"Yes you are, boy," he smiled, "Heh, heh, yes you are." I thought about what James had said and I realized that maybe he was right after all. Maybe this feeling of not belonging, of not being accepted was not my family at all, but me. Maybe I wasn't allowing those around me to accept me and then, I unfairly fostered resentments against others for that which I had brought upon myself. It was an intriguing theory that in a way empowered me. I thought that perhaps I was in control of my life after all. I began to feel less dread over this year's Christmas gathering. On the contrary, I was beginning to feel a bit excited. Here, I've wasted so much time feeling alone when all the while I have been surrounded by people who love me. Perhaps, I have not been the only one waiting after all. Perhaps, my family has been waiting as well, waiting for me. Grandpa had been the one remaining link that kept me from drifting away to a place that would not allow for my return.

"So, when ya headin' out?" James asked, bringing me back to my ladder from my head.

"Christmas morning," I responded.

"Well, good for you, boy. You just remember ol' James' theory, ya hear?"

"I hear, James," I said, and I truly did.

Chapter VII

I opened my eyes and turned toward the clock. Through the morning blur, I saw the time: 6:07. It was Christmas morning and I lay in bed, as I so often did, though this morning, I felt a sort of peace. "Good morning, Grandpa," I croaked, "Merry Christmas." I heard some movement outside my bedroom door and the doorknob squeak. I quickly closed my eyes so as not to be discovered as the first awake on Christmas morning. After all, I'm an adult now, right? I can control my excitement. I can sleep in on Christmas.

"Are you awake?" I heard my little sister whisper.

"Hmm?" I grumbled and rolled over in my best 'I'm asleep' fashion. I slowly opened my eyes and saw my sister beside my bed.

"Merry Christmas," she said when she saw I was awake.

"Merry Christmas," I returned as she sat on the edge of my bed. A mischievous grin spread across her face and I knew right away what she was thinking.

"Should we wake her up?" she asked. I laughed. I considered past Christmas mornings and my usual response to that question. Rather than asking my little sister to leave me alone and let me sleep knowing there would be no sleep, I felt a smile spread across my face as well.

"Yeah," I plotted, "Let's." She looked at me blankly for one surprised moment and the smile returned. I threw the covers back and together my little sister and me giggled and shoved our way down the hall to our older sister's room. I slowly and quietly turned the doorknob and pushed the door open just wide enough to poke my head inside. My little sister stood behind me gripping the back of my t-shirt and straining to see into the bedroom.

"I'm up," our older sister said, less than enthusiastically. My little sister, behind me was now leaping and dancing and trying desperately to muffle her laughter with her hands, so as not to wake our parents. Her reaction made me join in the laughter and we pushed our way into our sister's room closing the door behind us and suddenly the three of us were six years old again, laughing and shoving and whispering. It wasn't long before our parents gave up their fight for sleep; they were no match for the Christmas excitement that filled the house. Our father, draped in a bulky blue bathrobe, emerged from the bedroom rubbing his face. After a brief visit to the bathroom, he sleepily descended the stairs to the living room. Our mother followed shortly after and within a few minutes, though it felt more like a few hours, we could hear the crackle of the fire in the fireplace. Soon the sounds of Johnny Mathis crept up to the top of the stairs where we sat as if intentionally lined up according to age. That was our cue. As far back as I could remember, it was Johnny Mathis who called us to the living room each Christmas morning. Our excitement shot down to our toes and carried us scurrying down the stairs to the magic that awaited in the living room. Good morning kisses and Merry Christmas exchanges were followed by the opening of gifts. Happy sounds of laughter and love accompanied the Christmas carols rounding out the experience. I looked at my family. I found that I was feeling full of gratitude and blessings. My mother looked up from unwrapping a present that had been gloriously decorated by my father. She smiled at me and she was more beautiful than I had ever noticed. My smile answered hers and we shared a special moment that was never spoken of, somehow making it all the more special. My father looked first at his wife, and then at his children. He was swollen with pride and love and it poured from his soul as I watched. My father caught my eye and he winked at me. The love of my family was unconditional.

We turned into the freshly plowed driveway at Grandma's house around eleven o'clock that Christmas morning. There was a light dusting of snow blowing over the asphalt as a fresh dusting fell from the sky. In the front window, the warm yellow light beckoned and the earliest of guests shuffled about. We awkwardly pushed the door open with the open bags of gifts in tow. Inside the house, Christmas was alive. The smells of Grandma's culinary artwork tickled my nostrils, teasing my appetite and the air was filled with sounds of family. If I took the time to listen, to isolate each sound from the goulash of seemingly meaningless noise, perhaps I would hear young cousins laughing and fighting, and laughing again because they couldn't decide which was more fulfilling at the moment. Or, I would hear my uncle telling a joke, or maybe a story about his latest project in the garage and the laughter that always seemed to flow from his immediate vicinity. I may hear moms, spanning generations, scolding their children, or babying them as seen fit by the eyes of the eternal mommy within each of them. And of course I would hear the sounds of subtle disagreements, never quite developing into arguments, between the grown-ups who tried desperately to hide their annoyance behind forced smiles--all the while, their toes curling inside their shoes. Like I said, the sounds of family. What beautiful sounds.

I hesitantly approached the 'manly-man club' where they stood by the Christmas cheer. I was feeling a bit uncomfortable and was about to sneak away in the tradition of my little sister's great dinner table escape routine when my uncle reached out and smacked his hand onto my left shoulder and gave it a squeeze. I opted to stick around for a spell and actually had a few words to add to the exchange from time to time. After laughing at a few jokes and eating a few peanuts, I excused myself and moved on. I walked up behind one of my aunts as she leaned over the nativity with the other women. Placing my arm around her shoulders, I offered a half-hug and placed my head on her shoulder. She placed her arm around my waist and we stood silently and observed the beauty that Grandma created. I softly kissed my aunt's cheek and broke away from our bond. Walking down the hallway, I could hear the rustle of papers and giggles of joy coming from the TV room. As I rounded the corner, there they were, just as I remembered them, on all fours digging through the layers of

Christmas beneath the tree. They glanced up just long enough to see who had caught them in the act, offered a quick 'hello' and it was back to the hunt. I smiled and shook my head in amusement and remembrance as I took in the magnificence of the tree that appeared to embrace the cousins. Lights twinkled and decorations glistened in their glow. Then I saw it. The shiny glass Christmas ball that I knew so well. It was funny though, I looked and I looked but it was nothing but another silly ornament.

I returned to the commotion of the family celebration. Standing on the edge of the kitchen, careful not to get in the way, I tugged at Grandma's apron tie and she turned around. I started to open my mouth and Grandma just nodded with a tear in her eye and as she hugged me tight, I knew Grandpa was right, I had nothing to feel guilty about. I glanced into the living room and the empty chair that sat just outside the Christmas playing field. I didn't have to sit this one out, I thought. I'm okay. I'm really okay. Turning away from the sidelines, I returned to the game.

Chapter VIII

"So, you gonna tell me, boy?" James inquired.

"Tell you what?" I said despite the fact that I knew precisely what he was asking.

"How was your Christmas? I'm dyin' over here!"

"It was actually great, James," I laughed.

"Well, what happened between last week and today to make room for that musical laughter, boy? It's important that you be aware not only of this fresh, exciting feeling, but of what led you to it, dig? If you're ever to understand and to truly appreciate where you're at, first you gotta dig on how you got there," he explained. "You get what I'm sayin? You have to face the rough stuff, put closure on it." I looked at James. I could feel his radiating warmth and genuine compassion. I was ready.

"I was angry, James. I was angry and lonely. I've been waiting for a long, long time," I explained.

"I see. What have you been waiting for, boy?"

"I don't know exactly. I just haven't felt right for a long time, James, ya know? Then when Grandpa died, I was so confused. The only thing that made any sense was gone. I felt guilty and alone and so undeserving of Grandpa's pride, even of his love." I was trying desperately to explain myself. "Am I making any sense at all?"

"Perfect sense," James said softly.

"I wondered if Grandpa had any idea how much I always loved him, how important he was--is--to me. I still wonder." I felt a tear escape my eye and rush down my face as if running from the cold. It left behind a wet streak on my cheek, inviting the cool air to race in and nip at my skin. The sensation felt deceptively like heat burning my cheek rather than the frigid reality of the winter air.

"He knows, boy." Here we stood in the back yard, James looking into me rather than at me. I felt the weight of his strong hand on my shoulder. "He knows," he repeated. I squeezed my eyes closed, my eyelids acting as squeegees clearing the pain from my clouded vision. "Your old granddad is happy where he's at, Eric. He wants you to know that he is there watching and protecting you and your family. He's okay, boy. You're okay."

"But how do you know all this, James?" I insisted.

"I think you know how, boy. I know you do," James responded. I knew that he was right. I dropped to my knees so emotionally exhausted, I was unable to support my own weight any longer and welcomed the soft, cool purity of the snow.

"James, I just feel so..." I tried to grasp the appropriate words and then realized that I had already said them. "I just feel."

"That's it, boy, that's it, ain't it beautiful?"

"Yes, oh, God, yes!" I began laughing while the strength slowly found its way back into my body. I thought of the waiting room where I so often sat in my head, and I went back there for one final visit.

I sat in one of the chairs that lined the walls in this cold, dark, sterile room. I didn't sit long before I heard a door creak open. The bright light that poured from beyond the door engulfed me and then I heard it. I finally heard it: "Come on back." And so I did.

I opened my eyes. The image of the big, tattered work boots was a welcomed sight. I raised my head, looking up to James. The large man eclipsed the sun and appeared as a faceless shadow, but despite this fact, I knew he was smiling down on me.

"Your granddad is a good man, Eric, and you're a good grandson." The shadow continued, "You've always been a good boy and though I know you're not always sure of yourself, you always do what you believe in your heart to be right. That's all anyone can ask of you, boy." I felt so relieved, like a great lie had just been set free by the all-powerful truth. James reached down with one of those large, powerful hands and took mine. He helped me to my feet. "Stand tall now, boy," he said, "You don't live down there anymore. Stand tall and show the world what color your Kool-Aid is!" I laughed. I did what James said. I stood tall, it felt good, right.

"Now, c'mon, boy, we got a lotta work to do!" We climbed our ladders and resumed our work. We didn't speak; we didn't need to. I pulled off my bulky winter gloves and rubbed my eyes. For the briefest of moments, I felt a pain in my left forefinger. I looked to the site of the sudden pinch of pain and upon close inspection, found a splinter embedded beneath the skin. I remembered fondly, my "dream". I smiled. I don't believe I was ever before, nor would I ever be again, so happy to have a splinter. As I listened to James happily humming away, I glanced in his direction. I noted where James stood on his ladder, where I stood on my own and discovered that there was no longer a gap between where I existed and where the rest of the world existed. The rest of the workday floated by while I entertained thoughts about my family, about my life. I was able to appreciate the thoughts and the feelings they produced rather than challenging and analyzing them. It seemed as if no time had passed when suddenly...

"Clean up!"

We picked up around the yard and packed our tools in the truck. James tossed a smile in my direction, "Wanna ride?" he asked.

"I know," I said, "Your truck is right over there, right?" I responded sarcastically.

"You know it, boy!" He said and we walked toward the old pickup truck at the curb. We waved to the boss and were on our way. The ride was short and silent. We came to a traffic light that turned red and the truck squeaked to a stop. James nodded toward the bus stop. "Well, it was nice to meet ya, boy," he said offering his hand.

"What do you mean?" I was confused. "I'll see you tomorrow."

"No," James explained, "the job is done."

"But the boss said you can stay on," I argued against the inevitable.

"That's not the job I mean, son," James said and again nodded toward the bus stop.

"Don't go and miss your bus now." I accepted his hand in my own and felt the power and warmth that I felt the day we met. I opened the door and began to climb out into the street. "Watch your noodle," James said. He winked, so quickly I wasn't sure if I saw it at all. I felt a tear come to my eye as I pushed the door shut and backed away bending down to look into the open window of the truck.

"I love you, Grandpa," I whispered. "Goodbye." The light turned green and James drove off. James drove off and Duke Ellington played a happy tune in my head and all was right with the world.

◆

Author's Note

I am a first-time author. Needless to say, I have never before been in a position to write an "Author's Note". Therefore, I am not quite sure what is expected and so I decided to attempt to offer an understanding of where this book came from; from where I am confident more will come.

I know I am not alone when I say I have played host to troubled times. I know I am not alone when I suggest that these troubled times helped to mold me into the man that I am today. It is as if I am only now beginning to bloom. I once felt lower than dirt, but I now realize it is here where I had to plant my roots, drawing strength and nourishment from the very dirt that once suffocated me. I am here now to share with you the fruits of my struggles because I know that they are not MY struggles but OUR struggles.

Thank you so much for sharing this experience with me. I am very excited to have been granted the opportunity to tell this story with the hope that it has in some way touched you, made you smile. Consider this your invitation to join me again..."The Job" is only the first step of a journey, for I have much more to share.

Eric Whitfield
Greenville, NC, August,2001

Books from Science & Humanities Press

HOW TO TRAVEL—A Guidebook for Persons with a Disability – Fred Rosen (1997) ISBN 1-888725-05-2, 5½ X 8¼, 120 pp, $9.95 **18-point large print edition** (1998) ISBN 1-888725-17-6 8¼X10½, 120 pp, $19.95

HOW TO TRAVEL in Canada—A Guidebook for A Visitor with a Disability – Fred Rosen (2000) ISBN 1-888725-26-5, 5½X8¼, 180 pp, $14.95 MacroPrintBooks™ edition (2001) ISBN 1-888725-30-3 7X8, 16 pt, 200 pp, $19.95

AVOIDING Attendants from HELL: A Practical Guide to Finding, Hiring & Keeping Personal Care Attendants 2nd Edn—June Price, (2001), accessible plastic spiral bind, ISBN 1-888725-72-9   8¼X10½, 125 pp, $16.95, School/library edition (2001)   ISBN 1-888725-60-5, 8¼X6½, 200 pp, $18.95

If Blindness Comes – K. Jernigan, Ed. (1996) Strategies for living with visual impairment. 18-point Large type Edition with accessible plastic spiral bind, 8¼X10½, 110 pp, $7 (not eligible for quantity discounts— distributed at cost with permission of the National Federation of the Blind)

The Bridge Never Crossed—A Survivor's Search for Meaning. Captain George A. Burk (1999) The inspiring story of George Burk, lone survivor of a military plane crash, who overcame extensive burn injuries to earn a presidential award and become a highly successful motivational speaker. ISBN 1-888725-16-8, 5½X8¼, 170 pp, illustrated. $16.95 MacroPrintBooks™ Edition (1999) ISBN 1-888725-28-1 $24.95

Crash, Burn and Learn—A Survivor's Strategy for Managing Change—Captain George A. Burk (2002) Principles of Leadership and Total Quality Management by Captain George Burk, inspiring survivor of a military plane crash, who overcame extensive burn injuries to earn a presidential award. ISBN 1-888725-59-1, 5½X8¼, 120 pp, $16.95

Paul the Peddler or The Fortunes of a Young Street Merchant—Horatio Alger, jr A Classic reprinted in accessible large type, (1998 MacroPrintBooks™ reprint in 24-point type) ISBN 1-888725-02-8, 8¼X10½, 276 pp, $16.95

The Wisdom of Father Brown—G.K. Chesterton (2000) A Classic collection of detective stories reprinted in accessible 22-point type ISBN 1-888725-27-3 8¼X10½, 276 pp, $18.95

24-point Gospel—The Big News for Today – The Gospel according to Matthew, Mark, Luke & John (KJV) in 24-point typeType is about 1/3 inch high. Now, people with visual disabilities like macular degeneration can still use this important reference. "Giant print" books are usually 18 pt. or less   ISBN 1-888725-11-7, 8¼X10½, 512 pp, $24.95

Buttered Side Down - Short Stories by Edna Ferber (BeachHouse Booksreprint 2000) A classic collection of stories by the beloved author of *Showboat, Giant, and Cimarron.*   ISBN 1-888725-43-5, 5½X8¼, 190 pp, $12.95 MacroPrintBooks™ **Edition**   (2000) ISBN 1-888725-40-0 7X8¼,16 pt, 240 pp $18.95

The Four Million: The Gift of the Magi & other favorites. Life in New York City around 1900—O. Henry. MacroPrintBooks™ reprint (2001) ISBN 1-888725-41-9 7X8¼, 16 pt, 270 pp $18.95; ISBN 1-888725-03-6, 8¼X10½, 22 pt, 300pp, $22.95

Bar-20:   Hopalong   Cassidy's   Rustler Roundup— Clarence Mulford (reprint 2000). Classical Western Tale. Not the TV version. ISBN 1-888725-34-6   5½X8¼, 223 pp, $12.95 MacroPrintBooks™ edition ISBN 1-888725-42-7, 8¼X6½, 16 pt, 385pp, $18.95

Nursing Home – Ira Eaton, PhD, (1997) You will be moved and disturbed by this novel. ISBN 1-888725-01-X, 5½X8¼, 300 pp, $12.95 **MacroPrintBooks™ edition** (1999) ISBN 1-888725-23-0,8¼X10½, 16 pt, 330 pp, $18.95

Perfect Love-A Novel by Mary Harvatich (2000) Love born in an orphanage endures ISBN 1-888725-29-X 5½X8¼, 200 pp, $12.95

MacroPrintBooks™ edition (2000) ISBN 1-888725-15-X, 8¼X10½, 16 pt, 200 pp, $18.95

Eudora Light™ v 3.0 Manual (Qualcomm 1996) ISBN 1-888725-20-6½, extensively illustrated. 135 pp, 5½ X 8¼, $9.95

The Essential **Simply Speaking Gold** – Susan Fulton, (1998) How to use IBM's popular speech recognition package for dictation rather than keyboarding. Dozens of screen shots and illustrations. ISBN 1-888725-08-7 8¼ X8, 124 pp, $18.95

Begin Dictation *Using ViaVoice Gold* **-2nd Edition**– Susan Fulton, (1999), Covers ViaVoice 98 and other versions of IBM's popular continuous speech recognition package for dictation rather than keyboarding. Over a hundred screen shots and illustrations. ISBN 1-888725-22-2, 8¼X8, 260 pp, $28.95

Tales from the Woods of Wisdom - (book I) - Richard Tichenor (2000) In a spirit someplace between *The Wizard of Oz* and *The Celestine Prophecy*, this is more than a childrens' fable of life in the deep woods. ISBN 1-888725-37-0, 5½X8¼, 185 pp, $16.95 **MacroPrintBooks™** edition (2001) ISBN 1-888725-50-8 6X8¼, 16 pt, 270 pp $24.95

Me and My Shadows—Shadow Puppet Fun for Kids of All Ages - Elizabeth Adams, Revised Edition by Dr. Bud Banis (2000) A thoroughly illustrated guide to the art of shadow puppet entertainment using tools that are always at hand wherever you go. A perfect gift for children and adults. ISBN 1-888725-44-3, 7X8¼, 67 pp, 12.95

Growing Up on Route 66 —Michael Lund (2000) ISBN 1-888725-31-1 Novel evoking fond memories of what it was like to grow up alongside "America's Highway" in 20th Century Missouri. (Trade paperback) 5½ X8¼, 260 pp, $14.95 **MacroPrintBooks**™ edition (2001) ISBN 1-888725-45-1 8¼X6½, 16 pt, 330 pp, $24.95

Route 66 Kids —Michael Lund (2001) ISBN 1-888725-70-2 Sequel to *Growing Up on Route 66*, continuing memories of what it was like to grow up alongside "America's Highway" in 20th Century Missouri. (Trade paperback) 5½ X8¼, 270 pp, $14.95 **MacroPrintBooks**™ edition (2001) ISBN 1-888725-71-0 8¼X6½, 16 pt, 350 pp, $24.95

MamaSquad! (2001) Hilarious novel by Clarence Wall about what happens when a group of women from a retirement home get tangled up in Army Special Forces. ISBN 1-888725-13-3 5½ X8¼, 200 pp, $14.95 **MacroPrintBooks**™ edition (2001) ISBN 1-888725-14-1 8¼X6½ 16 pt, 300 pp, $24.95

Virginia Mayo—The Best Years of My Life (2001) Autobiography of film star Virginia Mayo as told to LC Van Savage. From her early days in Vaudeville and the Muny in St Louis to the dozens of hit motion pictures, with dozens of photographs. ISBN 1-888725-53-2, 5½ X 8¼, 200 pp, $16.95

Sexually Transmitted Diseases—Symptoms, Diagnosis, Treatment, Prevention-2nd Edition – NIAID Staff, Assembled and Edited by R.J.Banis, PhD, (2001) Teacher friendly --free to copy for education. Illustrated with more than 50 photographs of lesions, ISBN 1-888725-58-3, 8¼X6½, 200 pp, $18.95

The Stress Myth -Serge Doublet, PhD (2000) A thorough examination of the concept that 'stress' is the source of unexplained afflictions. Debunking mysticism, psychologist Serge Doublet reviews the history of other concepts such as 'demons', 'humors', 'hysteria' and 'neurasthenia' that had been placed in this role in the past, and provides an alternative approach for more success in coping with life's challenges. ISBN 1-888725-36-2, 5½X8¼, 280 pp, $24.95

Behind the Desk Workout – Joan Guccione, OTR/C, CHT (1997) ISBN 1-888725-00-1, Reduce risk of injury by exercising regularly at your desk. Over 200 photos and illustrations. (lay-flat spiral) 8¼X10½, 120 pp, $34.95 Paperback edition, (2000) ISBN 1-888725-25-7 $24.95

To Norma Jeane With Love, Jimmie -Jim Dougherty as told to LC Van Savage (2001) ISBN 1-888725-51-6 The sensitive and touching story of Jim Dougherty's teenage bride who later became Marilyn Monroe.   Dozens of photographs. "The Marilyn Monroe book of the year!" As seen on TV. 5½X8¼, 200 pp, $16.95 **MacroPrintBooks**™ edition ISBN 1-888725-52-4, 8¼X6½, 16 pt, 290pp, $24.95

Copyright Issues for Librarians, Teachers & Authors–R.J. Banis, PhD, (Ed). 2nd Edn (2001) Protecting your rights, respecting others'. Information condensed from the Library of Congress, copyright registration forms. ISBN 1-888725-62-1, 5¼X8¼, 60 pp, booklet. $4.95 postpaid

Inaugural Addresses: Presidents of the United States from George Washington to 2008 -2nd Edition– Robert J. Banis, PhD, CMA, Ed. (2001) Extensively illustrated, includes election statistics, Vice- presidents, principal opponents, Index. coupons for update supplements for the next two elections. ISBN 1-888725-56-7, 6¼X8¼, 350pp, $18.95

Plague Legends: from the Miasmas of Hippocrates to the Microbes of Pasteur-Socrates Litsios D.Sc. (2001) Medical progress from early history through the 19th Century in understanding origins and spread of contagious disease. A thorough but readable and enlightening history of medicine. Illustrated, Bibliography, Index ISBN 1-888725-33-8, 6¼X8¼, 250pp, $24.95

Rhythm of the Sea --Shari Cohen (2001). Delightful collection of heartwarming stories of life relationships set in the context of oceans and lakes. Shari Cohen is a popular author of Womens' magazine articles and contributor to the *Chicken Soup for the Soul* series.   ISBN 1-888725-55-9,   8X6.5   150   pp, $14.95 **MacroPrintBooks**™   edition   (2001)   ISBN 1-888725-63-X, 8¼X6½, 16 pt, 250 pp, $24.95

Ropes and Saddles—Andy Polson (2001) Cowboy (and other) poems by Andy Polson. Reminiscences of the Wyoming poet.   ISBN 1-888725-39-7, 5½ X 8¼, 100 pp, $9.95

The Job—Eric Whitfield (2001) A story of self-discovery in the context of the death of a grandfather.. A book to read and share in times of change and Grieving. ISBN 1-888725-68-0, 5½ X 8¼, 100 pp, $12.95 **MacroPrintBooks**™ edition (2001) ISBN 1-888725-69-9, 8¼X6½, 18 pt, 150 pp, $18.95

Once in a Green Room: A Novel—Keri Baker (2001). After being raped and having an abortion while in college, a young woman struggles to deal with her feelings and is ultimately helped by the insights she gains from her special education students. Contact information for help groups throughout the United States.Part of proceeds contributed to RAINN. ISBN 1-888725-38-9, 5½X8¼, 160 pp, $14.95 **MacroPrintBooks**™ edn (2001) ISBN 1-888725-61-3, 8¼X6½, 16pt, 200 pp, $24.95

Science & Humanities Press

Publishes fine books under the imprints:

- Science & Humanities Press
- BeachHouse Books
- MacroPrint Books
- Heuristic Books

Science & Humanities Press

PO Box 7151
Chesterfield MO 63006-7151
sciencehumanitiespress.com
phone 636-394-4950
Fax 636-394-1381

The Job—Eric Whitfield (2001) A story of self-discovery in the context of the death of a grandfather.. A book to read and share in times of change and Grieving. ISBN 1-888725-68-0, 5½ X 8¼, 100 pp, $12.95 **MacroPrintBooks**™ edition (2001) ISBN 1-888725-69-9, 8¼X6½, 18 pt, 150 pp, $18.95

An imprint of			
BeachHouse Books www.beachhousebooks.com	**Science & Humanities Press** PO Box 7151 Chesterfield, MO 63006-7151 (636) 394-4950 www.beachhousebooks.com E-mail: editor@beachhousebooks.com		
Item	Each	Quantity	Amount
Missouri (only) sales tax 6.075%			
Shipping			$4.00
	Total		
Ship to Name:			
Address:			
City State Zip:			